*"Poetry that takes you by the hand
and leads you into the woods"*

FAWN PRESS

Contents

Praise for 'This is where I find the softest hurt'

Praise for 'This is where I find the softest hurt'

'This is where I find the softest hurt' is a gorgeous debut. The poems shed a critical light on the way our bodies shape-shift to fit societal standards, with 'skin like origami' that bends and folds into acceptable shapes. Jasutan writes with unwavering precision, striking a delicate balance between the body as something alien and unrecognisable, and simultaneously a vessel that is deeply tethered to who we innately are. It demands we view the body with nuance: equally disturbing, beautiful, and desperate to find home."

-Nabeela Saghir

"Jasutan's poetry glows with sensory detail and keen observation. The voice is serious, careful and deliberate but finds joy in unexpected places – a long distance, an eccentric gesture of endearment, a kitchen counter. After spending time with these poems an underlying theme emerges: the innate note of sadness in a celebration and, conversely, the pleasure in rueful recollection. But this is coupled, always, with a determination to be attentive, to make something lasting out of the impressions that glimmer out. A beautiful debut."

– Luke Kennard

Trigger warning

- *Pedophilia, sexual harassment in 'Can You Move Your Hand Please, I'm Trying to Disappear, Sorry and Thank You '*

- *References to OCD in 'I'm the most sterile'*

- *Death, body horror in 'Tragedy of One Body II'*

Morning Ritual

i.
Some mornings it looks like this: peeling
my body off the bed to reconnect
with the earth. Doing warrior poses,
disremembering this body as a labyrinth
of bones and pink muscles; I,
a statue tall and erect in the centre of Empire,
I, a temple made of gray volcanic stones
sitting with myself for centuries.
Moss makes my hair. I shake hands with
tree roots, hug the tree trunks. These mornings
make me feel good.

ii.
My lover
asks what I want
for breakfast and I say
you and when I see his
face I laugh and say eggs
and who knows love can
be encompassed in such
a tiny round thing that
only knows stillness
and how to be
reformed

iii.
Other mornings a weight of fluff settles
on top of me; a cloud the shape of my sister
laughing, screaming, plucking my hair like dandelions.
She takes a bite of my cheek – a piece of kue cubit
in between her short little teeth. Bangun, ayo bangun.
Wake up now. The sun's out. Ada bakmi
for breakfast. Ayo cepat makan
and play with me, maybe we can go swimming,
see our bodies melt in the pool
like blocks of butter under boiling water.

iv.
Some days I open my eyes and close them again.
My breath: a sound of fight.

Mouth: Tip Jar

Drop some tips through this piggybank hole;
        worn copper laden with thumbprints, a wear and tear sign
            hear it ring against the coins of my teeth – it sounds like

a sigh and a gulp. The epiglottis working hard
        flapping like a fan in a summer's day, the buzzing in my throat
            to prevent anything impure going down the airway.

My jar opens wide like palms during Our Father, psalms
        in a prayer ready to catch blessings in the form of God's saliva.
            My jar with the non-existing lid

only knows how to build condensation around its body,
        wet glass from lukewarm breath by tongue flicking
            tenderness in the shape of a half moon.

For that which has been filled forgets how to be empty,
        to thirst is to go down the wrong way. Down to the larynx
            and produce a shrill in place of space

where you can be alone with your loneliness
        without having to watch it amalgamate in the mouth
            and broken down with enzymes.

Yet, why does it feel so good?

What a contamination sliding down the oesophagus,
what a good thing that my jar doesn't know how to close.

Tragedy for One Body

After Emily Berry

ACT ONE

[It is a windy night. Lamppost is the only source of light. Alone, clothed, and naked at the same time.]

ME : It was durian season when it happened

ME BODY : These eyes captured the world in grains; blinding white light as sharp as durian skin

ME : Time is suspended in people's mouth, trapped in one's saliva

ME BODY : I observed how a limb says goodbye. Hosts a funeral for 50 million skin cells dying every day

ME : [starts crying] I was so small, I didn't know gratitude was shaped like poison

ME BODY : I saw breasts detached, like fruits plucked from a tree

ME : And I was alone. You left me alone

ME BODY : Gratitude brewed inside the viscera. This throat is a tower of toxic fumes

ME : You left me

ME BODY : Skin sinking into bellybutton, I don't get why you so badly not want to cry

ME : [angry] You left me

ME BODY : I don't get I don't get

ACT TWO
[Standing side by side, yet one is invisible to the other]

ME BODY : I've been waiting to be picked up from the bathroom floor
ME : I wish my world can shrink into the size of my bedroom
ME BODY : You left me
ME : And maybe I can drown under the flooring
ME BODY : You left me I'm sorry
ME : And I will no longer have to see eyes
ME BODY : I've been waiting
ME : Not this body, not this excessive-muscle-tongue-mistaken-for-synapses-bone-with-nowhere-to-go body

ACT THREE
[Alone as always]

ME BODY :

ACT FOUR
[A melody from childhood, from taking a bath for the first time inside the mouth of a child]

ME BODY :
ME :

Onde Onde / Tang Yuan

I bought rice flour. I bought pandan leaves.
I bought ginger I don't know
how to peel. Sesame seeds in the cupboard.

My earliest memory is a palm
opening to cushion a piece of dough.
How it had fit between hands
that never stop moving. Stamping yourself
into what you eat feels exactly like

this: fingerprints on the white
mixture, thumb-dented like how a sculpture
never forgets her maker. Now it's too late at night

and we are hungry and decide that
culture could not feed these bodies.

The pandan leaves sit forgotten at the back
of the fridge. They turn mouldy – the edges
blurring like a winter solstice sky
the first night they were forgotten.

I never know when to start cooking
so everything that I do is too late.

All I know is rewinding that video from 2014
a round table full of glutinous rice balls,
my sister with flour and food colouring on her shirt
while sweet soup smelling of ginger and sugar

13

boiled in the hot and damp kitchen.

My dad told me to just buy tang yuan this year.
No one knows onde onde here.
Maybe culture wears a different name,
no longer a round table
but a cash register
when you are not home.

How to Cook (Nibble) Your Mother

This is the story of (un)becoming,
the first memory of consumption.
How everything is parasitic
from nibbling what your mother has eaten
to drinking her water, until you put affection
in the equation and suddenly it's a sacrifice.

This act of cannibalism
began from biting your mother.
Building feasts of dead skin cells,
tough muscles, and jutting bones
that never point in the right way.
Sprinkle mother's tears, her sweat.
What holy seasoning.

This is the lesson of eating
with your ten fingers
scooping rice pulps that look like
her brain tissues. How you can mistake them
for your intestines that greedily push
everything down. How easy it is to confuse
the food and the devourer.

This is the lesson of cooking,
of separating life with (dis)jointed fingers,
that washing the leaves under cold water
before splitting them to sections.

How it has always been an act of taking
before becoming you before becoming
something else. What (un)grateful sprouting
child. What blessed flesh and blood.

This act of violence (love)
began from my eating you, Mother.

(Con)sent

Has any word turned powdery white
in your mouth, the syllables cold like a trigger,
a bullet rolling on your tongue, gunpowder
smelling like an apology?

Mom said desire doesn't look pretty
in bare skin, in sober honesty.
This is chastity slipped in your wedding dress.

Has any word sent you into your own death
so many times, your mind is drunk with wine
-coloured pain, the next few hours
the world is flashing hell-white?

Mom said submission looks desirable,
meekness is dainty.
This is holiness unwrapped with a mouth.

It is not my fault for tasting a word so many times,
figuring out every metal is not a bullet,
every pixel of me is not a landmine.

I just want tenderness in my own terms.

Can You Move Your Hand Please, I'm Trying to Disappear, Sorry and Thank You

In the elevator, the man's hands look like broken slanted rooftops.
Discomfort like wood chips from my dollhouse castle stuck on fingers,
they perch on my arm - his touch unlike my mother's.
He says *oh so soft.*
I stare.
My nanny looks down; the air between us becomes
the umbilical cord where pains of womanhood pass through
generations
like nutrients we feed our bodies.
(At home, I say *sorry,* but my body flakes like frost
so it doesn't reply.)

In the classroom, the man's hands look like a cow's joint
where it settles on my nape. I almost don't feel human anymore.
His fingers, slick, straighten my shirt's collar, crisp,
like restaurant napkins, neatly folded.
I wish I could curl just like that.
My teacher says *there you go.*
I say *thank you, and sorry.*
(At home, I don't say anything, but the mouth
on my neck says *it's wrong it's wrong.*
With skin like origami, body tucked to form a rose,
I can't hear anything.)

In my university room, the man's hand is too thick to slip into my
underwear.
I wonder where my skin cells fly from the graze of his fingers,
if they are still me upon his touch. If anything is still mine.
Like the man before, he says *you're so soft.*
This time I say thank you, *thank you, thank you.*
(At home that is not a home, my atoms don't want to be me anymore.
I didn't know it was this easy to disintegrate.
My nanny didn't tell me all you have to do is see a hand,
think of love,
and apologise.)

Hands: A Blessing

I had this dream where the birthmark on my left foot pulsed
and stretched - a blue-grey island, blurry on the edges.
When you reached to touch it, see if the mark spills
and stamp shadows along your index finger, it opens
its mouth and you fit in between its rows of teeth.
Suddenly I have a mark in the shape of your palm
on the inside of my elbow, cloudy like a breath.
A mark in the shape of your fingerprint by my rib
like a secret. In this dream I remember thinking
of diffusion, how I become a part of you
when you enter the room; my body learning
the air I breathe has known you first.
In this dream, I extended both arms high
like a tree and suddenly my fingers grew long
strong and curly like a bowl enough to fit a nest.
My nails ripen and warm and you sprang free
like tiny yellow fruits, fragrant and sweet.
In this dream, you still wanted to touch me
and I grew more hands the more you did.
One by my hip complete with all five fingers.
Another two on my neck.
Three more by my belly.

On a random night, I speak to my body

1. If love had a voice, you would be birdsong. Or rain. Or the wind gushing, calling. Your mother picking you up from the first day of school, a pack of pandan bread and an orange juice carton on her open hands. Your partner's breath on your neck at the break of a nightmare. Your stomach flipping followed by the captain's announcement that we have safely landed. That tiny hitch in your voice after every laugh, a way for me to know that you feel safe.

2. You taught me you don't have to be the grandest garden, but make sure you always have enough wildflowers for the bumblebees to come. There is always space for seeds, the beginning of new lives. Among grass swinging, curling, make space for the dogs running happily, barking as they zoom into the sun.

3. If care had a smell, you would be congee on a Sunday morning. Or bubbling soup; chunks of carrots and green onions and potatoes vibrating in the heat. Tenderized meat with oil forming on the edges of the pan. Broth that greets you early morning when you are sick, a bowl of apology, an offering for forgiveness.

4. There is beauty in that painting in the quiet corner of the room, always there for the lost ones. That painting with no lines and edges, only colours: the colour a mother sees upon her newborn's first cry, the colour behind a diver's eyes as they break out of the water, the colour of the sky on the first rain on a spring day. The colour that I see when I see you.

5. You have given me eyes to see waves break against shore. Fingers for butterflies to perch into, legs to bury deep into the earth. Mouth to say I love you among other things. Moles as a secret I exchange with my lover. Ribs that create hollowness that only knows how to be filled. Dear, you have given me a way to savour the world - let me show you how full you can be that empty feels like a word they speak from a distant land.

Ode to Hickeys

Pansies bloom under the skin; roots
across the collarbone; bruised middles;
drops of purple paint; yellow clouds
wisping the edges; girdles cramping
the pulsating centres. This is tender
elastic flesh; blood trapped and frozen;
the shape of gemstones; how the body
is a mine but not mine to extract. This is
a memory of another body; a mark
of another mouth; of cupid's bow
knowing how to inhale. This is
the body knowing how to give back;
how to store. The body's inability
to separate strangers from lovers;
blind toward that thin line
between affection and violence. The skin
is alive whether the heart
pulses like the early air of spring
or clashes like cymbals in an unmediated
orchestra. This is the body announcing
its existence; the skin testing its resistance;
the blood saying *I will not stop; despite all;*
this is not just you waking up; this is the body
springing; going to light; saying
good morning; *hello, hello.*

I'm the most sterile

I've been in years.
My body is temperature tumbling,
summer surrendering, expelling
heat to be infertile.

After you left, I still see your things. Maybe this is what happens if you don't move enough: dust building on your surroundings, outlining your shape, a space waiting to be filled. Maybe this is why we were always fighting. I scrub the floor, ruining that mould. I put my sheets in the wash. I rewash my plates and bowls and mugs and cups and utensils ten times so none of them remembers your lips. Your breath when you laugh mid-meal. The cells from the inside of your cheek. Your saliva.

As if I'm not clean enough
      I curl into a ball
in my bed. I don't want to shed
      in a space other than this.
I don't want my room
      to have skin cells
that have known you.
This is a promise

          I made to myself.
    I will live
        like a walking ignition
  for the next ten years.

Love used to feel like being spotless
yet not barren.
        So what do I do with the
breadcrumbs   dandelions   flower petals
 from my nails   from too much plucking   from expired
                                              memories

I can't keep cleaning.

        If I keep going

                        I will be gone.

this is not a poem

this is a body before burial / the brain coming to a rest / the cooling down after an assault / this is about stopping as gentle as skin drooping / about blood that only knows how to run / now is forced to stay mute / about wine-stained skin the shape of a spinal cord that looks like unbloomed wings / this is the human body as a tightrope / a cycle coming back to one last tension like a newborn curling / this is a body eating itself inside out / cells biting cells / microorganisms slurping cells / a feast of tissues and skin / falling of teeth / spilling like seashells from mouth / unspooling of ligaments like satin ribbons / nails like armour removed in moments of peace / this is a moment of peace / this is not a poem about my body / this is a body / unthinking yet inviting more lives / more communities to roam in these skeletal hotel rooms / empty chambers for more families to dine and dance and sleep and love in / this is a body turning off its overflowing tap / for once emptying doesn't feel like a sacrifice or a poem / but fulfilment

You're beautiful

After Princess Mononoke

Even under your feet life blooms like blood,
grass parts and mellows as you come running.
Guardian of forest, the mirror of trees,
I wonder what language you speak in your dreams.
If there is a word for I want it this much. If I will come undone
the way you renounce human and take up spirit princess.
If there is a metaphor to describe this: you cradled
in wolf fur, me wishing it was my arms.
A mountain of iron cannot make me rust the way
your name settling on my tongue does.

Your name: an invitation, a beginning to loving
only with my mouth, the only intentional parting
that knows of the uncurable hunger, like a knife
can never be sharp enough. Your name: a calling
for me to go under, palm first into the centre of the earth
where your heart beats with a thousand mouths open
ready to swallow. This is where I find the softest hurt,
needing you like a newborn reaching for his mother's
skin to know he's alive. My hands crumple to carbon and oh
would it be a crime to stamp your name with my soot
-stained fingers. Oh would it be a crime to unpluck a spirit
off its life-source just so I could live.

Skin: Rest Area

One night I trace the tail of a shooting star on your
dorsal hand, the scar light-bright
                    like a memory; a wish.

Sometimes I wonder if my touch leaves an imprint on your skin,
if it's as clear as protruding bones beneath komodo scale:
                    hidden but tough. Maybe you don't know
your fingerprints stamp like copper plates with batik motifs
        and my skin is a cloth with the thirst to absorb ink.

I wonder if you know that I like to play tourist
on the temple of your collarbone, where every step crumbles
                                    yet promises safety, sayang.

If you know your hair runs like the softest blades of grass
in between my fingers, if you know a prickling sensation that comes
from knowing there is life on the flowerskin you pinch, how its stem
    bleeds sap human tears.

How this overwhelming awareness of soul
saturates me like a blanket when I'm with you; this sea
drenched in salt, the feeling of blue sky when you're at Arupadhatu,
        and I'm always at Arupadhatu when you're here, sayang.
                            Istirahat, karena aku di sini.

One day my arms will crumble to andesite and regrow into purple orchids
my breath carving a silver star on your skin.

Self Portrait in Young Adult

The sky always tastes so salty, dusts over bed covers
over crumpled candy packaging over
dreams written on biology textbook – mitochondria
is the powerhouse of oneself. One day
the sun will not feel too bright and
cup well in a palm, shining in between fingers,
splitting like onion skin to reveal the same material
that builds a person. One day
we are no longer running and jumping and
dancing but counting days in a week
wondering if they still feel like weekends: sharp on the edges
but yield and soften upon touch.
One day Mama will ask, as always, *what do you want for dinner?*
That day we will say, *I know.*

Phantom Limbs

Not every distance is the cause of an amputation,
yet every kilometre – a phantom limb to hold.

i. mama
I did not tell Mama that I inhaled home from the reusable masks
she sent me. I greeted her arms in between
a blend of orange-lavender-sandalwood
essential oil – love as clean as detergent and touch.

> Iya, Mama masih pakai parfum
> yang biasa kamu pakai: udah
> tinggal setengah.

When I go shopping, I see her eyes staring
at my reflection. Mama knows what fabric
makes her tropical skin pulverize in the cold,
a sign of our own unbecoming.

> Mama beliin kamu baju
> kemarin dari pasar.

When I cook, she stands behind me.
A statement: waaah makannya udah kayak bule.
Eyeing whether the skin by my wrist
is still yellow, unwashed.

> Kita kemarin makan di
> restoran baru,
> nanti kalau kamu pulang kita
> pergi lagi, ya.

I wonder if longing is translatable through screen.

> 姐姐 pulang*, dong.

ii. abel

                                    I love you that I can bite your ear lol.
Yearning caused her to take a slice of pear to her mouth,
imagine it was my flesh – what can be felt under the teeth
cannot be unreal. These fruits become her way of reliving.
                            I wonder what it feels like touching
                            your face.
                            You're not home for a year.
                            Of course I forgot.
And yet here I am, every day imagining how her shoulder curves
like mangosteen against the arch of my palm.
Every tiny baby hair settling on her forehead
upon sleep – rambutan bristling in the heat.
                            姐姐 kapan pulang?
This is how I see ache reworded in screen.
                            姐 pulang, dong.
I keep these phantom limbs close until pulang is a –

*In Indonesian, we have a word for 'going home' – this verb is used the
same way as 'go', but only towards home. For the years I am not home, I
learn to think of home as the journey.*

Kitchen

For Yuri, Sophie, and Hannah

the hob:

>frozen meatballs bobbing up and down in bubbling broth
>swimming alongside wilting Chinese leaves and blocks of fried tofu
>with their white chambers heavy and filled with water & I
>remember you
>coming in and saying *this is just what I need* & I remember you
>saying
>enoki mushrooms have an earthy smell but we eat them anyway
>because we like how they break under the teeth & I remember
>your oldies music and how your movements match the shimmering
>of the broth: like waves in an erratic and rhythmic kind of way.

the counter:

>the smell of garlic washes over the kitchen and we peer
>lover bubbling cheese that pops and deflates & see the brown bits
>in between chopped parsley & the dough crisps
>on the edges. mozzarella sticks unmoving but hissing
>when taken out of the oven: hot to touch but soft and fluffy in the
>mouth
>and you say what a good evening to consume lactose. how do we
>combine coconut milk and Indian curry spices and pasta and
>somehow
>it still tastes heavenly; not entirely soup and not entirely cream
>but this might be what our friendship is like: flavours bursting
>in your mouth that go straight to your heart.

the table:

on Chinese New Year we fight for roast duck drowning in plum
sauce
& mistake purple yam for roast pork & eat noodles for longevity.
chopsticks as extensions of fingers reaching out for water chestnuts
and bamboo shoots, crispy beef and sauce-drenched chicken.
after dinner we snack on kue lapis & I think the Dutch preserved
butter
melts on my tongue & I think you said I remember this & I think
I thought why don't you come home with me. see srikaya ooze out of
buns,
pork floss gloss over bread & there is so much more I want you to
see;
the kitchen I grew up in, how similar
they are to our Thursday nights and our silly little meals.

Lunar New Year Feast

Dear red envelopes. Dear red dresses
and cheongsams and an auntie's laughter.
Dear pot of boiling soup with mushrooms
the shape of an ear, flower carrots
and fishballs like giant pearls. Dear kue raya -
crunchy tube-shaped cookies
broken and shared among cousins,
cat tongues that melt into buttery goodness
on the first contact with the mouth,
crescent-shaped cookies coating my fingers
with snow. Semprong, lidah kucing, putri salju.
Dear the prayer inside red envelopes
in place of money. Dear games amongst cousins.
Dear gossips from the family members
you meet once a year, only this time of the year.
Dear seconds for dinner. Dear there is always room for desserts.
Dear February rain. Dear Chinese music in malls,
in the streets, in your neighbor's house. Dear dancing
and karaoke. Dear the loudest and fullest day
of the year, my house bursting and open
to take in any distant relative in this hari raya.

To Die For

After Sam Smith

what is prettier
than the breath

                      a tongue

                              that does not hate the teeth

    one day I will meet someone

        they will part my bones and see

        the sun rising from beneath like a disk   I wonder

                              if that will come

                              before the mirror stares back

                what is prettier

                than the heart

                breathing   a self

                                      that unhates

                                        its ___

one day I will touch my neck
and find my necklace warm
because of my skin

                          I wonder

                          if that will come

                          before the mirror parts

                                          its teeth

what is prettier
than a mirror
unshouting   back   my thumb   beneath my wrist
                              my eyes.   not looking like disks

                                                           looking exactly like this:
                                                                     the breath

Acknowledgements

When I was little, I would fold A4 papers and staple them together to form a book. I would then write stories in my makeshift book, and that's how I started writing. There had been many makeshift books ever since, and my parents had to replace the pack of A4 paper very often.

Thank you to my dad who approached a publisher and self-published the first manuscript I finished when I was ten and to my mom who always reminds me that anything is possible for me. To my family, without whom I would not be here.

Special thank you to Isabel Galleymore and Luke Kennard, my professors and dissertation supervisors, who helped me shape the majority of the poems in this pamphlet - this book would not exist as beautifully without their guidance.

A large part of this pamphlet is deeply inspired by Ocean Vuong's Night Sky with Exit Wounds and Natalie Diaz's Postcolonial Love Poem, especially regarding the meditation of the body.

'Kitchen' is inspired by 'Kitchen' by Jay Bernard's collection Surge. 'How to Cook (Nibble) Your Mother' is inspired by Victoria Kennefick's collection Eat or We Both Starve. 'Tragedy for One Body' takes inspiration of Emily Berry's 'Tragedy for One Voice', with regards to a performance poem in the form of an impossible act.

'You're beautiful' is inspired from a scene in Studio Ghibli's Princess Mononoke. 'To Die For' has its title taken from Sam Smith's song 'To Die For'.

Many many thanks to my friends who continue to inspire me every day - Sophie, Yuri, and Hannah especially. Thank you to my best friend and partner Farrel. Thank you to my friends from home who continue to cheer me on until this moment - Andien, Matea, Levina, Chika, and Mitha. Special thank you to Andien for the beautiful illustrations and cover for this pamphlet.

Warm thank you to Mercy, Philip, and Christopher for being my family and making me feel at home in the UK since day one.

Thank you to the family at The Emma Press - Emma, Georgia, James, Kyaice, and Peri for the support of this pamphlet.

Thank you to my Editor Scarlett, for your guidance, friendship, and support in helping me bring this book into the world.

And finally, thank you for picking this book - I hope it leads you to light beyond the rubble.

About The Author

Christi is a Chinese Indonesian writer based in Birmingham and enjoys writing about the body, lived experiences, and food through experimental metaphors. She completed her BA in English and Creative Writing at the University of Birmingham and 'This is where I find the softest hurt' was born largely from the poems in her dissertation. Her work has appeared in harana poetry, Hungry Ghost Magazine, and streetcake magazine, among others. When Christi is not reading or writing, she can be found doing one of her many hobbies: cooking, baking, crocheting, yoga, aerial fitness, or rewatching Studio Ghibli films.